Prairie Dog

AT HOME ON THE RANGE

WRITTEN BY SARAH TOAST
ILLUSTRATED BY RON MAHONEY

Publications International, Ltd.

Beneath the surface of the windblown prairie is a whole town of burrows that have been dug by prairie dogs.

Baby Prairie Dog was born in the spring. He has eight sisters and brothers and too many new cousins to count. Their burrows are connected to other families' burrows in the underground prairie dog town.

In the clear, cool night, a few deer and elk gather. They graze where the antelope and prairie dogs grazed during the daytime. Beneath the deer and elk, Baby Prairie Dog sleeps.

The danger has passed, but a summer cloudburst soon soaks the prairie. The burrow mound, which serves well as a lookout post, also keeps the rain from flooding the burrow.

Baby Prairie Dog and all his brothers and sisters and cousins play together in the snug, dry burrows while the rain pounds above them.

Father Prairie Dog stands on the burrow mound, keeping watch while the prairie dog pups are grazing. Looking toward the rain clouds, he sees a hawk.

Father Prairie Dog yips and barks, and all the inhabitants of the prairie dog town scurry into their homes. Father Prairie Dog barks until the hawk comes near, then he dives for safety.

By the middle of the summer, sunflowers are starting to bloom. Later, Baby Prairie Dog and the others will gather the sunflower seeds and enjoy a feast.

Prairie dogs become very fat during the summer so they can survive the lean winter months when there is very little grass to eat and grasshoppers cannot be found.

After their first two days out of the burrow, Baby Prairie Dog and the other pups begin to eat the same foods the grown-ups eat: the leaves and roots of wiry grasses, and grasshoppers.

Pronghorn antelope graze next to where the prairie dogs graze. The antelope are not disturbed by the noisy bouts of chattering and playing.

Father Prairie Dog and the other adults take turns watching for their natural enemies: ferrets, coyotes, bobcats, and badgers.

Rattlesnakes and bull snakes are also dangerous to the prairie dog families. And prairie dogs fear birds, too. Hawks, falcons, and eagles fly overhead scanning the ground below and hunting for small animals.

Each burrow has two entrances that provide fresh air and safety. Father Prairie Dog tends a small mound of soil around an entrance. He will stand there to look out for danger.

Baby Prairie Dog interrupts his father's work one time too many, so his father thumps him with his paw. Baby Prairie Dog finds another playmate.

Baby Prairie Dog and the other young pups follow the grown-ups everywhere, trying to get them to play. Mother and Father Prairie Dog enjoy playing with their pups. They let Baby Prairie Dog climb all over them.

All the grown-ups are friendly to each other and to all the pups. They groom one another while they chatter and play.

For five long weeks, Baby Prairie Dog and his brothers and sisters snuggle with their mother, as they nurse and sleep. Their eyes haven't opened yet.

After they open their eyes, the pups can go above ground. Baby Prairie Dog sees the green grass and the blue sky. He sees the grown-up prairie dogs greet each other by rubbing noses.